Contents

GROWING IN GOD'S GRACE AND REVIVAL

My True Story on My Redemption in God's Plan!

Jasmine Lopez

ISBN 979-8-88851-690-4 (Paperback)
ISBN 979-8-88851-691-1 (Digital)

Covenant Books
11661 Hwy 707
Murrells Inlet, SC 29576
www.covenantbooks.com

Chapter 1

YOUR IDENTITY

I will commence by stating, "All praise, honor, and glory to my Abba Father God, His Son and Prince of Peace, Jesus Christ, and the Holy Spirit (The Trinity) for guiding and providing me with the spiritual intel to press forward with the wisdom and strength to articulate my story."

Following the voice of God is the cornerstone of every minutia and facet of my life.

As I embark on this journey of sharing my personal testimony, exposing the darkness, and illuminating the presence of my Lord and Savior Jesus Christ's infinite love, now I can reveal my truth. These four scriptures have been monumental in my story:

> Who knows, perhaps you have come to your Royal Position, For Such a Time as This. (Esther 4:14)

> But you are a chosen generation, a royal priesthood, a holy nation, His own special people, that you may proclaim the praises of Him who called you out of darkness into His marvelous light. (1 Peter 2:9)

> She is clothed in strength and dignity and
> laughs without fear of the future. (Proverbs 31:25)

> Then you will know the truth, and the
> truth Shall Set You Free. (John 8:32)

Inherently, I am continuously thriving to elevate my testimony and all the ways the Lord Jesus has brought me through the crossfires so I may have a platform to testify where I am today.

I tell myself that each day is a gift, a treasured gift from God, a new day that will flash before my eyes, in the blink of an eye. Then as each day passes, I find myself asking, "What did I do today to glorify God's kingdom? How did I share the gospel? Did I make a conscious effort to not sin?"

With all these fluttering questions, I take a step back and remind myself we are all created in God's image. I am not perfect, I make mistakes and fall short of God's glory, so why am I condemning myself?

I strongly believe we all may fall into these traps and clever schemes from the adversary, the deceiver, the evil one, the thief in the night, Satan. He is the supreme spirit of evil, and his personification is rebellion, pride, deception, and many other wicked attributes.

> Put on the full armor of God, so that you
> can take your stand against the devil's schemes.
> (Ephesians 6:11)

Truth be told, I have struggled with my identity my entire life and only until recently, I truly learned that I was created in the image of God. I believed that my image was a culmination of the level of education I attained, my successful career, being above the status quo, chasing the money dreams, vanity, idolatry, pride, and never melting into the crowd. I surrounded myself with material possessions my entire life and defined my self-worth by "creating my own image."

> Put on your new nature and be renewed as you learn to know your Creator and become like him. (Colossians 3:10)

> He must increase, but I must decrease. (John 3:30)

> God is all-knowing. (Daniel 2:20–22)

I have no doubt that my Lord Jesus has set me free from this bondage, and only He can keep me humble, so thank You, Jesus, for this part of my salvation and inheritance. While you're reading these words, please know that Jesus can set you free from any fear, bondage, tormenting thoughts, anxiety, sadness, strongholds, and depression. You are connected to the one who created you, all praise and glory to our King Yahweh for His faithfulness and unwavering love. He is the light of this world!

In your walk with the Lord, basking in the light of his glory will take you to new heights that are sustainable and coupled with abundant peace.

I encourage you to read the scriptures daily and allow the Holy Spirit to guide you on your precepts and completely surrender to the Lord Jesus.

Along with surrendering and spiritual hunger, you will feel the love, solitude, and embrace of His love permeate through every part of your spirit.

There is nothing more rewarding than feeling true peace, joy, love, and kindness flowing in your life, and the best part is sharing it with your family and friends. Lastly, continue to take inventory of your life as it pertains to the body of Christ and allow the Holy Spirit to show you areas of your life that will exemplify God's grace and mercy. All of it will resonate with you so you have wisdom, knowledge, truth, and pure expectation of God's power within your spirit to do what is holy and acceptable in His eyes for full kingdom advancement.

> But the fruit of the Spirit is love, joy, peace, patience, kindness, goodness, faith, gentleness, and self-control; against such things there is no law. (Galatians 5:22–23)

> If we live by the spirit, let us also walk by the spirit. (Galatians 5:25)

Chapter 2

YOUR OBEDIENCE

Throughout my spiritual journey, I have come to the realization that to have a deeper relationship with my Lord Jesus Christ and to continue to elevate to a deeper and higher level with Him, I must always remain humble. Now that may not be the easiest stance to take but think of it this way, when you're making decisions in every area of your life, isn't it better to take a step back, take a deep breath, pray without ceasing, and talk to God first?

I have encountered so many times when I think and act impulsively, my outcome in the situation can either be a success or a failure, so why take that risk? I rather air on the side of cautionary measures, not judging others or being irrational but rather looking at it through a spiritual lens. We must come from a place of humility and, more importantly, obedicnce.

When you hear that little voice inside you, helping you before you jump into the next decision, always remember that is the Holy Spirit guiding you on your path to a decision that pleases God.

Being obedient in the moment and using discernment to make a clear and concise choice that will manifest into a positive outcome. Sometimes we may just have a sinful consciousness and act on our feelings, but just know that is temporal. So before saying the wrong words, being spiteful or prideful, sending a rude text message because you want to have the last word, etc. Adhere to the Holy Spirit, take a step back, inhale/exhale, and talk to our Lord Jesus and ask Him first, "What should I do?"

Simply, repositioning yourself to listen to God's voice and trusting Him will ultimately be the best decision since we are the righteousness in Jesus Christ. Hallelujah!

Prayer is when you talk to God, and meditation is when you're listening to God. When I meditate on God's biblical word or find a quiet place to pray, I am reassured of God's omnipresent love.

Furthermore, we will endure seasons in our lives where we will experience hardship, unexpected moments when life is blissful, and all of a sudden, you're faced with a difficult situation, and you may go through a season of darkness or a season of sadness, but always remember, so did our Lord Jesus. He faced the same opposition from the devil, so He wholeheartedly understands the battles you come up against. It is very apropos to say there is nothing He can't turn around in your life. I emphasize the word *grow* because it propagates the rhetoric of abundance, full and sustainable joy, that ebbs and flows through us like the living waters of a majestic ocean.

> Jesus replied, "Anyone who loves me, will obey my teaching. My Father will love them, and we will come to them and make our home with them." (John 14:23)

> Resist the devil and he will flee from you. Draw near to God and He will draw near to you. (James 4:7–8)

Chapter 3

GOD'S PERFECT TIMING

For many are called, but few are Chosen.

—Matthew 22:14

What would profit a man to gain the
whole world, but to lose his soul.

—Mark 8:36

This is one of my favorite Bible scriptures since it denotes so many aspects of my life when I knew I had areas of opportunities to build up my faith and when I was tested during trials and tribulations. Realistically, I thought I was ready for certain breakthroughs and encounters; equally, I was struggling with demonic bondage, unfortunately believing the devil's lies when I knew better.

My prayers were answered, and some were not, only until now as I evolve with learning more about the gospel and God's perfect timing is when I knew God was always the cornerstone through my journey and strengthening my spiritual maturity. I'm grateful that I am yielding to the word of God because every ounce of power that the devil has is rooted in a lie. Tell yourself to break the lie! Your trials will birth triumphs, and you don't need to live in condemnation. If you're going through a sinful consciousness, humbly come to God's throne and repent of your sins, and you will feel the full transparency of His forgiveness, unceasing peace, and agape love.

Praise God, hallelujah!

It wasn't always easy navigating through the challenging times, and I had to learn and differentiate what was my purpose and calling versus adapting to a self-fulfilling prophecy.

I struggled with the carnality of my own selfish desires and falling into the devil's snares, which resulted in a prideful state of mind.

Well, all I must underscore is we are not conformed to "this world" (Romans 12:2), and there is always an outpouring of our Lord Jesus encapsulating an omnipresent love all around us.

Once I truly surrendered it all to Jesus, I yearned to commune with Him and build more of a relationship with Him. Holiness is ownership! That's what Jesus showed me; inherently, we have the birthright authority and the free will to either submit to God's commands or turn from Him and subject ourselves to the unknown.

I've never been much of a risk-taker, but there is something alluring about taking a deep dive into a decision that may or may not be in my favor and, unequivocally, a momentary impulse. Likewise, thank You, Jesus, for the Holy Spirit and the many gifts bestowed such as wisdom, discernment, counsel, and the fear of the Lord so I may not live in a fool's paradise.

Personally, I have discovered there is no way to be legalistic when it comes to following spiritual disciplines. We have the far greater, Most High, anointed King of the universe, Jesus Christ, and His endless love for us, which gives us the reassurance that we are His beloved! Hard times may leave us in darkness, but they can never separate us from His powerful light!

When you're feeling shipwrecked, alone, struggling with depression or sadness, lamenting in those negative thought patterns, allowing Satan to continue fueling his lies, etc., give yourself grace! Pray to our Abba Father God and remember you're His chosen one!

Through this supernatural awakening are His perfect timing to align His faithful promises, a myriad of blessings, and complete restoration. His promises are yes and amen!

This world is temporal, a vapor, and it will not be a part of our eternity. We must embrace our mission to always give and let our light shine before others so that we glorify God's presence and his purpose in all divine moments. Our Lord Jesus exemplifies judicious loyalty, and receiving salvation is a gift!

When I was baptized at the beach, I placed my entire faith in God more than ever! I was cleansed and sanctified, a holy awakening and refreshing through my spirit and publicly professing my faithful commitment, that my God-given purpose was to praise His holy name, stand on the mountaintop, pick up my cross, and be a bold daughter of the King of kings and Lord of lords, Yahweh!

My hope is for everyone to grow in Christlikeness! There is freedom in God's love!

Jesus loves you!

> Here I am! I stand at the door and knock. If anyone hears my voice and opens the door, I will come in and eat with him at the table, and he with me. (Revelation 3:20)

> I have come as Light into the world, so that everyone who believes in Me will not remain in darkness. (John 12:46)

> Let us continually offer to God a sacrifice of praise—the fruit of lips that openly profess His name. And do not forget to do good and to share with others, for with such sacrifices God is pleased. (Hebrews 13:15–16)

> For the word of God is living and active, sharper than any two-edged sword, piercing to the division of soul and of spirit, of joints and marrow, and discerning the thoughts and intentions of the heart. (Hebrews 4:12)

Chapter 4

Encouragement

Every single day is a gift, and I want you to feel encouraged and know that when you put your full faith and trust in our Lord Jesus, you are connected to the one who created you and His unwavering love and a blissful experience, a true manifestation of jubilation, clarity, and serenity in your thoughts. Hallelujah!

Once a manifestation of your innermost desires is supernaturally led by the Holy Spirit, pray for patience, so the appointed time is revealed. Sometimes we only have one chance in life, and we want the best outcome.

I know God is designating the best plan for my life, and He will do the same and even more for you! King Jesus far surpasses our expectations with His mercy, grace, and insurmountable love.

Reading your Bible daily, speaking the powerful word, which plants and waters the seed will ultimately produce a harvest. Enjoy the process while you're waiting for your harvest; additionally, faith is our operating vehicle while you're experiencing patience, diligence, and becoming deeply rooted in God's wonderful garden of life.

Words of encouragement

The gospel is the proclamation of God
The word of God is sown into our hearts
God's vision is our provision in our lives

We are the righteousness in Jesus Christ
He crowns us with confidence
He throws your sin in the sea of forgetfulness
Being a child of God comes with a badge of honor
Transformation is the next step toward deliverance
Purification and sanctification is a part of inner healing
Spiritual growth brings Christian fellowship and a zest for life
Repentance manifests a changed mindset which builds intimacy with God
We are crowned *royalty*—don't have a blind faith, come boldly to the throne of grace with your prayers
Activated faith will be your contact point to our Perfect Messiah, Yahweh
Don't do it in your own strength, trust God's plan

> Trust in the Lord with all your heart and lean not on your own understanding: in all your ways submit to him, and he will make your paths straight. (Proverbs 3:5–6)

> He calls me beautiful one. (Song of Solomon 2:10)

> Be still and know that I am God; I will be exalted among the nations. I will be exalted in the Earth. (Psalm 46:10)

> And now the prize awaits me, the crown of righteousness, which the Lord, the righteous Judge, will give me on the day of his return. And the prize is not just for me but for all who eagerly look forward to his appearing. (2 Timothy 4:8)

❧❧❧

Chapter 5

REVIVAL

You cannot have revival without repentance, and when you pray faithfully, then you become a carrier of the glory. We decree and declare that our purpose is to accomplish the assignment that is destined for all of us. That we shall bare fruit (love, joy, and peace), and this is conditional to all the spiritual disciplines aligned in God's scripture reading.

A very important part of my deliverance process was when I started fasting. Prior to pulling down strongholds, repenting from my sins, and rededicating my life to Jesus, I learned about incorporating fasting in my spiritual breakthrough. Once I experienced the breakthrough, then I felt the full transformation. An awakening from God's anointing (the anointing breaks the yoke, Isaiah 10:27) followed by the outpouring of God's divine nature, which encompasses your spiritual gifts, an inheritance, and a double portion of restoration and revival. Glory to God!

You're no longer operating in your own carnal flesh or making decisions based on worldly nuisances. We have the birthright authority to proclaim our gifts and remind ourselves that we are not earthbound; more importantly, we're radically changed, and God is calling you to decree and declare in your victory!

Fasting and prayer

I encourage you to be a prophetic visionary and pray about how you can encounter your spiritual breakthrough. Pray about the type of fast our Lord wants you to start and how long it will be.

For example, I completed the twenty-one-day Daniel fast, and I was able to recognize idols that I needed to eliminate in my life coupled with a seven-day water fast prior to my baptism.

Both fasts were rewarding and refreshing and solidified the biblical truths that brought me back to humble beginnings and spiritual growth. It's all part of my deliverance!

When you fast and pray, it restores and strengthens your intimacy with God.

Fasting is not a chore. Fasting is not part of your to-do list this month. Fasting is not a "recommendation or a solution to a problem."

When you humble yourself and commence with the power of fasting, you're saying, "Okay, my Lord Jesus, I want more of Your presence, stir up my faith, increase my spiritual hunger, and decrease my worldly desires."

Your flesh goes down, and your spirit is lifted high. I felt amazing spiritually, mentally, and physically! Rejoicing and praising our author and perfector, King Jesus!

> So we fasted and petitioned our God about
> this, and he answered our prayer. (Ezra 8:23)

> Fasting will loose the bands of wickedness,
> undo the heavy burdens, let the oppressed go
> free, and break every yoke. (Isaiah 58:6)

> Be thankful. Let the word of Christ dwell in
> you richly...as you sing psalms, hymns, and spiritual songs with gratitude in your hearts to God.
> And whatever you do, whether in word or deed, do
> it all in the name of the Lord Jesus, giving thanks to
> God the Father through him. (Colossians 3:15–17)

Chapter 6

A Sound Mind

A sound mind is wisdom sharpened by the word, no blurred lines, and God's vision, which is far greater than our sight.

An intimate relationship with our Lord Jesus is a multifaceted approach of conduit prayer, worship, and transcending faith. When we co-labor with Him to obey His commands and consecrate ourselves (consecrate, "submission and declaration for a divine purpose"). This is fortuitous since our Lord Jesus, our Chief cornerstone, and His perfect timing is yielding to the sovereignty of God. We start to recalibrate our lives by simply loving God with all our heart, soul, and mind, so we have His protection and preservation united with His desire and coming into alignment with our spirit. I always remembered that "worship is warfare."

Thank You, Lord Jesus, that you continue to pour into us fresh oil, fresh revelation, and unyielding love. We are seated in heavenly places!

Beautiful and poetic scriptures from Psalms:

> The heavens declare the Glory of God, and
> the sky above proclaims his handiwork. (Psalms
> 19:1)

> When my heart is overwhelmed, lead me to
> the rock that is higher than I. (Psalms 61:2)

> For the Lord God is our sun and our shield.
> He gives us grace and glory. The Lord will with-
> hold no good thing from those who do what is
> right. (Psalms 84:11)

God is committed to His purposes, not our formalities of this world, and we should hold ourselves to a standard of grace, not perfection. Furthermore, we partner with God to disarm the enemy, and our holiness is ownership, which demonstrates practicalities and ideologies ruled by God.

In this effort, we must have a mindset, which incorporates to live by faith, walk in love, and grow in grace. Again, we receive impartation from the anointing, which is flowing, when we surrender to God's will, our God, Jehovah Gibbor Milchamah (Psalm 24:8).

The anointing is never disappointing, and the anointing destroys the yoke (i.e., bondage), and in Matthew 11:28–30, Jesus invites all who labor and are heavy laden to come unto Him, take His yoke upon them, and learn of Him.

We are all given the kingdom keys—victory, dominion, freedom, power over the enemy, and redemption. We were designed by God, for God, so as you're making choices, remove any negative, carnal habits, repetitive indoctrinations from your mindset, and don't get stuck in the silos. We are not under the curse, you must believe, with every fiber of your being. Beloved God will avenge you and set you free from the chains that are holding you down from your sins.

God gives us:

- Love (God is love, John 4:8)
- Hope and future (Jeremiah 29:11)
- Freedom (Romans 12:2)
- Grace (James 4:6)
- Wisdom (James 1:5)
- Faith (Romans 12:3)
- Rest and sleep (Psalm 127:2)
- Victory (1 Corinthians 15:57)

There will always be propaganda all around us from political to social and spiritual agendas that will continue to arise on a global level. Social media platforms, TV/radio, and other media outlets are the catalyst for stirring up a web of lies and salacious, entangled, and fabricated stories.

Simply unsubscribe from anything that is a source of dissension and contention; sometimes you must be legalistic in the choices you're making. Avoid coming into agreement with certain words. These could be identified as word curses that you're speaking over your life, e.g. "I wish I could be more like this person," well, this is called covetousness or a continuous negative mindset, habitual patterns, i.e., addictions, envy, jealousy, greed, vanity, etc…

We are not earthbound, and God will not placate our carnal thoughts. Never lose hope and always continue to forge ahead and plug into the Bible every day!

As you have higher levels of encounters in your life, metaphorically speaking, always remember, there's nothing new under the sun; in laymen's terms, history repeats itself.

When you have a holy encounter, be progressive with that experience. God blesses you with a breakthrough, so then He requires more from you and expects you to multiply it and bless others.

In Luke 12:48, it states, "For everyone to whom much is given, from him much will be required."

We need to set our minds on the word of God and be on a spiritual movement that showcases our God-given talents. We all have gifts and special talents; it's God's kaleidoscope of love that He imparts to all His children.

While I was attending church service, God gave me an impartation of the PART method. Prayer. Application. Redemption. Transformation.

I was in His glory and intimately in spiritual exchange with Him as He made these deposits of the PART doctrine. In the moment, I wanted to burst out in a song as I always do when I have a heavenly encounter. It's amazing how He meets us where we are. Similarly, when our Lord Jesus came down from the cloud and spoke with

Moses (Numbers 11:25), I also felt the power of His glory radiate through me.

I want everyone to apply this method in their lives and become prosperous!

I believe it's imperative to always remain humble and exhibit invigorating faith, pray without ceasing (never stop praying), exercise obedience, and most importantly, I would implore you to apply the word of God and read your Bible with an open heart.

God occupies the space in your life, and His love and grace are inescapable…it's ever-present.

Despite Apostle Paul begging for that "thorn in his flesh" to be removed; therefore, we must append to Jesus and His mighty strength, which trumps our weakness. The pure confidence we have in our identity is the acceptance of Jesus abounding with fruitful love. We are chosen!

Let us pray for grace to grow in our effort to consider one another, and as it states in one of my favorable Bible verses, "Lead a life worthy of your calling. For you have been called by God" (Ephesians 4:1).

In the book of Genesis 28:10–28, Jacob had a dream and saw the ladder of heaven, the ladder symbolized "stepping up" into a different dimension, and it represents ascension, substantial increase, and reaching a higher level of connection between man and God. The Lord appeared to Jacob, saying, "'He was the God of Abraham and the God of Isaac' [Genesis 28:15]. 'Know that I am with you; I will protect you wherever you go and bring you back to this land.'"

This scripture inspires me because I want to rise and soar on an elevated level with God and faithfully honor Him! To testify is to prophesize in God's imperial expansion of His word and don't allow anything to crush your spirit!

The best part is we all will live confidently, testifying that we have the inherent beauty of God, and we should embrace it. We can be radically changed, and I strongly believe that grace is the weapon that disarms the darkness, and only by His grace, we are saved.

In summary, we all have imperfections, but I love the scripture, "We are perfectly imperfect" (2 Corinthians 12:9).

> Let us consider how to stir up one another to love and good works, not neglecting to meet together, as is the habit of some, but encouraging one another, and all the more as you see the Day drawing near. (Hebrews 10:24)

> But as for me, I will watch expectantly for the Lord; I will wait for the God of my salvation. My God will hear me. (Micah 7:7)

> The Kingdom of God is within you. (Luke 17:21)

> You have been chosen to live in freedom. (Galatians 5:13)

Chapter 7

DISCOVERING YOUR PURPOSE

As born-again, new believers, this would be part of a new gospel movement called the discovery phase, where people start to develop their spiritual disciplines, new identity/new creation in Jesus Christ, and grow spiritually with the sword of the spirit, the biblical word of God.

Another element of this movement is learning your spiritual gifts and how they align with your purpose and calling.

I believe the most important part of this is building intimacy with God because people are no longer conformed to this world, but they're renewed and transformed in their minds (Romans 12:2).

Born-again Christians and Christlike believers growing in their journey must realize that their walk with God is different from others, and they need a starting point, which we know is reading the Bible and other ways to strengthen their relationship with Jesus Christ, embrace your grace, and always have sustainable faith. The best part when you're navigating through your journey is you start to bare fruit such as love, peace, and joy, as it is written in the scripture (Galatians 5:22) so that you may plant seeds and serve others just like Jesus did when He was living on the earth.

We are set apart and are to live a contrarian lifestyle, we are unique and gingerly created, and God does not make mistakes. I love the scripture in the Old Testament in Jeremiah 1:5, "I knew you before I formed you in your mother's womb. Before you were born, I set you apart and appointed you as my prophet to the nations."

It's such a remarkable way to continue to plant in faith, every season of your life, and throughout any struggles or circumstances you may encounter, you're not alone in a crowded room. Our author and perfector, wonderful counselor, Yahweh is right there guiding you.

> For I am not ashamed of the gospel, for it is the power of God for salvation to everyone who believes. (Roman 1:16)

When I delved into my purpose after so many months of going through various nesting stages, I knew I needed to make a conscious effort to truly become radically changed. God dropped spiritual deposits in my spirit and centered my life in more ways than I could ever dream of. He is the God of the impossible, and He always surpasses our expectations. I was purely struggling with being double-minded (we cannot be double-minded in our ways). I quickly learned from watching pastoral sermons, reading revelatory biblical information, and immersing myself in prayer that a double-minded person is unstable in all their ways; therefore, there is no discrepancy in your prayers (James 1:8).

We must stand in our authority and claim healing, deliverance, freedom, etc...

After many divine interventions, I changed my approach, and I would speak with boldness and robust prayers and stay on a narrow path, focusing on God, not just asking over and over but seeking His response first so that I may listen to what He has prepared for my life. It's paramount that we're in a constant posture of watchfulness and prayer. God will unpack it all—you will proclaim over your life and receive breakthrough, restoration, deliverance, seeds of God's goodness, and inner healing coupled with spirit-led worship so you learn about your discipleship, being equipped in his word and being in alignment with God's divine assignment!

A purpose without God's plan is just a dream!

I purchased journals and prayed to God and asked him, "Father God, what is my purpose in life?"

I heard God's audible voice, and He said, "Write down five things that you want to accomplish."

I eagerly wrote down the following:

- A deeper relationship with my Abba God, King Jesus, and the Holy Spirit
- Find a great church where I can have deliverance and more freedom
- Water baptism on the beach
- I want to sing for Your glory and write a song
- Write my testimonial book so I may be the light and help others

Supernaturally, I felt God's glory all through my spirit. It felt as if beautiful butterflies were fluttering through the air, and I could see in the heavenly places, and I just praised God over and over, as tears streamed down my cheek. I said, "Thank You, God, thank You, Jesus, for loving me."

He meets us where we are, and His love overflows like the rivers of living waters. It was the Holy Spirit's presence, my hope of glory, pouring out the providence of my new destiny.

The greater one is in all of us!

I knew I was destined to be in a life of some type of ministry. My purpose now is to help transform people who are abandoned, in despair, serving other gods, backsliding, and spiritually attacked.

In the spirit realm, there is no time or limitations; however, I always felt as if I'm running against the clock, or there's never enough time to accomplish my daily list, but God quickly showed me that all my efforts are part of serving His kingdom, and I will work on the five things I asked for so I may purposefully acquire what is righteous for His glory and share the gospel through singing, writing, serving my church community, and communing with Him one hour at a time and one day at a time because we are on God's timetable, and each precious day is a gift.

Those who are wise will shine like the brightness of the heavens, and those who lead many to righteousness, like the stars, forever, and ever. (Daniel 12:3)

Each one must give as he has decided in his heart, not reluctantly or under compulsion, for God loves a cheerful giver. (2 Corinthians 9:7)

The voice of the Lord is upon the waters; the God of glory thunders; the Lord is upon many (great) waters. The voice of the Lord is powerful; the voice of the Lord is full of majesty. (Psalm 29:3–4)

You gave me life and showed me kindness and in your providence watched over my spirit. (Job 10:12)

Chapter 8

MY SPIRIT IS INDESTRUCTIBLE

How I conquered demonization with the power of Jesus

Before I start with this part of my testimony, I will be authentic in every detail and obedient in my description as I discuss the intricacies of what I experienced from a demonic, spiritual state of mind and the physicalities of what my natural eyes and ears saw and heard in the spirit realm.

The level of interactions my mind, body, and soul experienced were encounters that no human being should ever endure! The best way for me to describe this time in my life was I entered a spiritual atmosphere, a living nightmare and hell on earth, which pivoted into a dimension where I knew I was "never going to be the same again."

We all have a spirit, we have a soul, and we live in a body.

I spiritually shifted into where I will implore you to keep an open mind that this was a season of my life that every part of my soul and my spirit was consumed by the fire of the enemy, yet through it all, God carried me through and never left me. Glory to glory!

God didn't set me up for failure; rather, I count my blessings more than ever because he saved me from the gates of hell, a pit of tormenting darkness full of death, the smell of sulfur, decay, and destruction. When I was going through demonization, unbeknownst to me, I entered the devil's full access territory, and I allowed it. The countless nightmares of visiting hell, astral projections of demons all around, day and night, objects moving around my house, and the worst of it all, not feeling the love of God.

The reasoning behind this is when you choose your sinful carnal flesh desires such as divination, idolatry, etc…

The spirit world now has full access to gain legal rights over you as well as a history of bloodline generational curses of witchcraft. These principalities and powers are on a mission to destroy God's people.

I never knew why, but now I understood the depths of my actions, for example, watching scary movies, listening to certain types of music, which I identified with as well as coming into agreement with these ideologies.

Your spirit can be exposed to the "ways of this world," and if you don't have discernment, there is a demon/familiar spirit or a spirit of deception/monitoring spirit that is coming against you. My whole life was breached, and I had to go into self-preservation mode. My spiritual hunger kicked into overdrive. I grabbed my Bible, I literally took my cross, and I knew I needed to go on the mountaintop and fight with the birthright authority I was given. Praise Jesus!

I thought I was a bulletproof Christian, and I could feel the pulse of God, but it took a very long time for me to become radically changed. I had a group of prayer warriors who stood in the gap for me, specifically, my husband, who never stopped fighting for me. I am so eternally grateful to be married to a mighty and strong prayer warrior. A few pastors were on the frontline interceding with prayers, but we faced many challenges and opposition from our local churches who resisted helping me.

My mother was so deeply involved in my day-to-day tormenting struggles. I will just say that her prayers and unrelenting love were so greatly appreciated. Her strength through it all was more than any mother could endure; lovingly, she cared for me and carried me through so much, not knowing what I was really going through. I will be forever grateful to her. I love you, Mom!

My other family members, my mother-in-law, and my brother-in-law were saving graces as well from the inception of when it unlocked all the mental sufferings and spiritual warfare, their ongoing prayer and covering were blessings that symbolized God's shield of favor and protection. I love them both so very much.

The reality is there is a spiritual war we are battling, and we must be warriors who will be progressive in prayer, interceding for the nonbelievers, taking up our cross for more breakthroughs, awakening, and outpouring of God's consuming fire.

We must take a deep dive into fighting back against these spirits of witchcraft, deception, generational curses, strongholds, water spirits of the marine kingdom, and draconian agendas and forge ahead in receiving higher levels of encounters, as it states in Matthew 12:34, "Out of the abundance of the heart, the mouth will speak."

In this day and age, we cannot have a lukewarm gospel or be passive with our stance against the diabolical schemes integrated on a global level. Truthfully, in my humble opinion, I have determined the cultural movement, which transcends on all platforms: social media, television, radio, etc., and most of it is not rooted and grounded in love, and the worst of it all, there is no reverence of God.

I'm compelled to tell this very morbid part of my testimony because as I type the words, I feel freedom and deliverance of every part of my testament, and walking through my deliverance daily, I know it's imperative to exercise prayer, read my Bible, and come boldly to God's throne with worship and praise.

Every day I tell myself to leave no stone unturned, seize the day, and celebrate every serendipitous moment because God is our oxygen, He is the sunrise, He is the sunset, and I would have no existence without Him. I fully comprehend the world we live in and all the judgments from people that cast a net in our opinions and decisions, and we must be in pursuit of God and embrace our grace. I once heard someone say, "If you fall for people's praises, then you will die by their criticisms."

In summary, don't believe the lies the devil brings you. He's convincing you of this because he wants you to think you don't have freedom. Simply, we must reject the devil and command the attacks to stop in Jesus's name. The lies demons put into your thoughts perpetuate a hysteria of confusion, and they pretend to make you think you're trapped forever. Rebuke it and fight back with the word of God.

Thank You, Lord Jesus, for Your breakthrough, warring angels, and Your army of ministering angels who protect us from the enemy's relentless attacks.

Be proactive and declare your truth in Jesus's almighty name, and Satan and his demons must flee as you command the name of Jesus over your life.

Repentance is required every day for our sins and transgressions. These scriptures truly sustained me through deliverance:

> Behold I give you the authority to trample on serpents and scorpions, and over all the power of the enemy, and nothing shall by any means hurt you. (Luke 10:19)

This is the truth about the Abyss/the Lake of Fire:

> Hell has a lake of fire. (Revelation 19:20, 20:15)

> There will be no escape from hell. (Matthew 25:46)

> Hell is a place of torment and torture. (Luke 16:23)

> There will be weeping and gnashing of teeth. (Luke 13:28)

Chapter 9

GRATITUDE

Noteworthy is the fact that heaven is the pinnacle!

We are welcomed into the light for all eternity, as it states in Isaiah 43:19, "See, I am doing a new thing and we will see him face to face when we get home."

When I think about my forever home, *heaven*, I think about seeing all my loved ones, in this forever place of utopia, filled with light, love, and endless joy with praise and worship.

We serve a mighty, majestic God!

There is nothing better than having an eternal state of mind, and we know one day we will see *Jesus* face-to-face and have the privilege of spending eternity with Him.

Let us take those who are downcast, despondent, and in utter depression and lift them up for increased spiritual health. My mission is to always have full transparency and acknowledge that we must show ourselves grace and gratitude and let our light shine before others so that we may glorify God's presence.

Gratitude is the origin of worship!

My heart takes flight knowing that I will live contrary to this world and be more compatible with Jesus.

I learned through many prophetic pastors and apostles that repentance is correction, which is interwoven with doctrines that advance God's kingdom and fortify us to become valuable, yielded vessels. We're overcomers! We are the righteousness in Jesus Christ, so let's stay encouraged by reading the scriptures and hearing God's voice.

When you're birthed in the fire, you won't settle for the smoke!

I believe God will save you first, then he will deliver you because the miracle is in your journey, not in the moment.

Furthermore, allow God to ignite your fire since you won't grow and thrive in your comfort zone.

The enemy rushes us, and God leads us; so tap into your inner spiritual strength, and God will order your steps along the way.

God will do the heavy lifting, so read your bible with expectancy. We all will receive our redemption, and it shall come to pass.

Where there is pain, there is a purpose. King Jesus comes to bind up the brokenhearted, and we can feel the pulse of God if there is a spiritual hunger to zealously seek His kingdom first!

We want miracles, signs, and wonders while serving others, which God loves a cheerful giver. When I speak my love and prayer language of tongues, there is an acceleration of growth.

Let us get back to God's original design.

We have citizenship in heaven, we are immersed in our Lord Jesus, and we are the righteousness in Him. Always position yourself to decree and declare it over your lives!

I'm awestruck by the amount of gratitude I have for all my family, brothers, and sisters in Christ who interceded and stood in the gap for me. I am forever grateful for them!

I am free, I am loved, and I will never allow the enemy and his minions to hold me captive. Jesus came to set the captives free. Amen!

Encouraging scriptures to say every day:

He makes beauty from ashes. (Isaiah 61:3)

> Now to Him who is able to do exceedingly abundantly beyond all that we ask or think, according to the power that works within us, to Him be the glory in the church and in

Christ Jesus to all generations forever and ever. (Ephesians 3:16–21)

If we confess our sins, he is faithful and just and will forgive us our sins and purify us from all unrighteousness. (John 1:9)

Your word is a lamp to my feet and a light to my path. (Psalm 119:105)

Behold, I am about to do something new; even now it is coming. Do you not see it? Indeed, I will make a way in the wilderness and streams in the desert. (Isaiah 43:19)

Let the words of my mouth, and the meditation of my heart, be acceptable in thy sight, O LORD, my strength, and my redeemer. (Psalm 19:14)

The fear of the Lord is the beginning of wisdom and the knowledge of the Holy One is understanding. (Proverbs 9:10)

But you have come to Mount Zion and to the city of the living God, the heavenly Jerusalem, and to myriads of angels. (Hebrews 12:22)

His yolk is easy and his burden is light. (Matthew 11:30)

For the word of God is living and active sharper than any two-edged sword. (Hebrews 4:12)

Chapter 10

PERFECT PEACE

Growing up in Brooklyn, New York, I use to take the train to high school, actually, multiple trains since the journey was over an hour. The best part of the commute was looking out the window after the sunrise permeated throughout the sky and staring at the brightness of the illuminating sun. A wonderful array of bright orange and yellow colors, just my sweet reminder that I get to live another day, and I always knew in my heart God was with me. It was our moment together before my school day commenced. Every second spent with God floods my life with love, harmony, and exuberance.

A spectacular view filled with love, hope, and perfect peace. Over twenty years later, I will carry this sunrise moment together with my Father God. His infinite love surrounds me like the warm sun. I knew in my heart I will never be alone, I don't have to be afraid, and I am fully protected and cared for throughout my entire life.

Essentially, the train ride was indicative of my journey, growing in grace on the path that I knew God would lead me to. I believe what was unveiled to me on how *big* my *God* is in every area of my life. Growing in His grace and His mercy and endless love.

Lord Jesus gives me the grace to grow in freedom to answer my calling.

> The Son is the dazzling radiance of God's splendor, the exact expression of God's true nature—his mirror image! (Hebrews 1:3)

> We are Chosen and Loved by God. (Ephesians 1:4)

Rapture in His Majesty forever

Even then at sixteen years old, there was something so tangible about the large sun radiating in the sky, the quiet silence on the train, my eyes set upon God, and this intimate connection we had together. He is the Prince of Peace, Yahweh, our Perfect Peace.

You're never alone. There is an inheritance your heavenly Father left for you so pick up your mantle and run the race until Jesus returns!

> They overcame by the blood of the lamb
> and by the word of their testimony. (Revelation 12:11)

Nothing missing, nothing lacking, nothing broken
– Shalom –
Peace be with you
The King is coming.

My Sunrise Moment with God

A Lotus flower symbolizes rising from a dark place
into beauty, rebirth, and wisdom.

GROW IN GRACE

BY FAITH

Closing

For from his fullness we have all received Grace upon Grace. (John 1:16)

May all who love you be like the sun when it rises in its strength. (Judges 5:31)

I have found the one whom my soul loves. (Song of Solomon 3:4)

Blessed is she who has believed that the Lord would fulfill His promises to her. (Luke 1:45)

Blessed be the God and Father of our Lord Jesus Christ, who has bestowed us with favor and spiritual gifts. To know him is the highest, richest, and most rewarding aspect of our whole relationship with him!

Be encouraged every day and always have faith.

Salvation Prayer

Lord Jesus, I repent of all my sins, and I surrender to you, Lord God. I believe and declare in my heart that Jesus died on the cross for the forgiveness of my sins and rose on the third day.

By faith, I receive you as my Lord and Savior Jesus Christ.
Thank you for making me a new creation.
In Jesus's almighty name, I pray. I am saved by your grace.
Amen.

For God so loved the world that he gave his
one and only Son, that whoever believes in Him
shall not perish but have Eternal Life. (John 3:16)

A Vision for You

What do you feel God is calling you to do?

What role would you say faith plays in your life?

42

Where would you like to grow with your spiritual gifts?

I love you all beyond words.

May God richly bless your pursuit of His divine plan!

Love and blessings!

Always,
Jasmine

Jasmine is on a mission to grow and bloom in her journey to proclaim that we all can rejoice that we all have inheritance and deliverance from bondage.

Her passion to encourage others is also lived out through her profession as a marketing entrepreneur within the state of Florida where she resides with her husband, family, and amazing friends! She loves meeting new people and sharing the love of the gospel!

She enjoys songwriting, singing, and is launching her collection of uplifting songs.